The Way of Repentance

Irma Zaleski

NOVALIS

CONTINUUM • NEW YORK

© 1999 Novalis, Saint Paul University, Ottawa, Canada

Published in Canada by Novalis, Saint Paul University, Ottawa, and in the U.S.A. by the Continuum Publishing Company.

Cover design: Blair Turner
Cover icon: "The Resurrection of the Just" painted by Brother Claude Lane, OSB
Layout: Chris Humphrey

Novalis, 49 Front St. East, Second Floor,
Toronto, Ontario M5E 1B3   (416) 363-3303

Canadian Cataloguing-in-Publication Data

Zaleski, Irma, 1931-
The way of repentance
ISBN: 2-89088-980-7
1. Repentance--Christianity. 2. Repentance--Orthodox Eastern Church. I. Title.
BT800.Z34   1999   234'.5   C99-900007-1

The Continuum Publishing Company, 370 Lexington Ave.
New York, NY, U.S.A. 10017-6503

Library of Congress Cataloguing-in-Publication Data

Zaleski, Irma
   The way of repentance / Irma Zaleski
      p.   cm.
ISBN: 0-8264-1158-4
   1. Repentance--Christianity.   I. Title.
BT800.Z35   1999   98-53157
234'.5--dc21   CIP

Printed in Canada

CONTENTS

PREFACE

It is hard for most contemporary men and women to understand and accept the need for repentance, not just as an occasional pious exercise, but as a constant attitude of heart and a *way of life*. At least, it has been so for me. The understanding of repentance, which I acquired as a child and accepted unthinkingly for many years, was limited to an experience of *regret* – of being sorry – for the sins I had committed. The regret was often quite genuine, and even painful, but there was a simple and familiar way of dealing with it. To return to the state of innocence and to be "good" again, it was only necessary to confess my sins and ask forgiveness for them. Anything further than that I tended to view with suspicion, and considered inappropriate for our more "enlightened" age.

But life has a way of teaching us to expand our vision and to face reality on its own terms. As I grew older, as I continued to try and live the life of faith and struggled with my own weakness and inability to do so, as I failed again and again at being "good," I began to realize that, beyond my obvious, daily sins, there lay a deeper reality and a more profound sense of sorrow. I came face to face with what the Fathers of the Church called *the root of all sin*: separation from God.

This sense of separation from God, of being *exiles from Paradise*, the longing to return to it, and repentance as the way we must take, lie at the heart of the whole Christian Tradition – East and West. Yet this seems largely neglected and obscured in the recent religious practice and the liturgical life of the West. Perhaps, because we think of repentance in terms of *guilt*, we find it difficult to open ourselves to it. There are not many who can understand repentance as it should be understood, as a way of healing from guilt and of *liberation from self*. Those who do are fortunate, but they have few companions on the way and even fewer teachers or guides.

In my own life, it was my introduction to the practice of the Jesus Prayer and an encounter with the Tradition of the Eastern Church which helped me to understand the source of my inner sorrow and pointed the way to its healing. It led me eventually to the door of the great mystery of repentance, the mystery of God's infinite mercy and love. It is about this mystery that I have tried to write here. This is not meant to be a book of theology or a discussion on ethics, but a short reflection on what I believe to be a central teaching of the Faith and a way in which all of us – saints and sinners – can embrace and live it.

FOUNDATIONS

The call to repentance is fundamental to the whole Christian Tradition. It echoes throughout the Old Testament and lies at the very beginning of the New. John the Baptist, the Precursor, was sent to summon the people to repentance – to a *conversion* – that is, a *re-turning* to God. Christ himself called for repentance as the condition for entering the Kingdom (Matthew 4:17) and, when he sent out his disciples on their mission, he gave them the same task (Mark 6:12). After Pentecost, the Apostles preached "life-giving repentance" – repentance which leads to life – as a necessary condition of salvation. Repentance was the sign of the presence of the Holy Spirit in the pagans and opened to them the grace of baptism (cf. Acts 11:18). The early Fathers of the Church, the Councils, the saints, countless thousands of the faithful believed and tried to live out this call. How is it possible, then, that so many contemporary

Christians – at least in the West – seem unable or unwilling to hear and answer it?

There are two main reasons for this, I think. First of all, perhaps, we no longer understand the real meaning of repentance. We do not often understand it in its true *religious* sense, as a way of love and freedom, of total trust in God's infinite mercy. Instead, we tend to view it in mainly psychological terms: as a negative emotion or state of mind, an expression of an exaggerated, even neurotic, *sense of guilt*.

Secondly, because we often do not understand the nature of salvation, we do not realize the immensity of what we have lost as a result of sin. We cannot, therefore, mourn the absence of what we do not know we could have. In fact, we do not understand the true nature of sin. We tend to think of it as disobedience, the breaking of this or that commandment, individual wrong acts, rather than as a painful *condition* of the human spirit, a shadow background of all our lives. Thus we are inclined to view repentance as a way of paying a debt, a spiritual "transaction," and do not easily see it as a way of healing and life.

GUILT

The many tragic and destructive consequences of guilt as a psychological condition have impressed themselves upon us. The term *guilt* suggests a state of mind associated with childhood trauma and neurotic self-hate. The roots of it often lie in our subconscious and are difficult to bring to the surface, not easily accessible to our understanding or will. Guilt in this sense is a terrible burden which many of us carry for much of our lives. Often we feel we can bear it no longer: it tears us apart, destroys all hope and joy, and makes us fearful, unable to trust. It is only right that we should try to rid ourselves of such a terrible, soul-destroying burden. In the life of a Christian, guilt in this sense should have no place.

Yet it is a tragedy of many Christians, especially older ones, that this painful sense of guilt has been encouraged and confirmed by misguided teaching which they received during their religious education or heard preached in church.

3

They may have been taught to fear God's anger and to doubt the unlimited nature of his mercy. They may have been made to feel hateful, unworthy of love, no good. This is a dreadful distortion of the healing message of the Gospel and the life-giving repentance to which it calls us. From that perspective, it is not difficult to view repentance as a way of self-punishment and self-hate. This is a terrible and dangerous misunderstanding, and an obstacle to many on their way of salvation. The repentance to which we have been called is not a way of self-condemnation and guilt, but the way of our *healing from guilt.*

Guilt, however, can also be understood in a much more limited, more positive sense. It can be viewed as our *natural* response when – in the presence of God – we realize that we have indeed done wrong, that we have hurt another person or ourselves, that we have acted against our own true nature (that is, against the image of God in which we were created), and have contributed to the evils which torment our world – in other words, when we have realized that we have committed a sin. It is right, even necessary, to feel guilty in such a situation.

But guilt in this limited sense – awareness that we have sinned – should never lead us to self-hate or depression. Further, this realization should not be confused with that deep and bitter agony of heart which is often referred to as "remorse."

Remorse is usually understood as a deep, never-ending "biting" of guilt, a gnawing agony over what one has done in the past, perhaps many years ago. This kind of remorse is not only psychologically unhealthy, but can also be spiritually destructive. It is a clear sign of our lack of faith in God's power to forgive sin and to take away the burden of guilt from us, once and for all.

Instead, the awareness that we have sinned should lead us to what the Christian Tradition calls *compunction* – an acute realization of our responsibility for something we have done or failed to do, and of our need to confess, to ask forgiveness and to make amends. Compunction, in its literal sense, means a *pricking*, a quick, clean piercing through of the heart by the awareness of a wrong committed. True compunction, although it makes us aware of our sinfulness, makes us also deeply aware of God's infinite, constant willingness to forgive. Compunction is a sign of *trust* and not of despair. It removes the burden of guilt from us.

This does not, of course, mean that we should forget our past sins, blot them out of our minds and pretend that we have never committed them. "Forgive and forget" can be misleading advice. We learn from experience. The consequences of our sins will remain with us, perhaps forever, and we must never forget that we have committed them, and are capable of committing them over and over again. True compunction will make us ever more aware of this truth, ever more alert to the temptation to sin, but it will also teach us to surrender ourselves totally to God's mercy and to be at peace. It will make us ready to receive the grace of true conversion of life and heart.

CONVERSION

The early Fathers of the Church used the Greek term *metanoia* for "repentance." It means *conversion* – literally, "a change or transformation of the mind." (This is not our rational mind, but the "inner" mind, or the heart). *Metanoia* means the "waking-up" of the inner self to our true condition before God and our response to this grace, that is, our returning – not just once, but again and again – to the path of holiness. For a Christian, the path of holiness must always mean an unending struggle to live the life of love: love of God, love of neighbour and true love of ourselves. Because we fail in love and are most often centred on ourselves, we must always repent – turn back to God – and ask for forgiveness, again and again.

If we can grasp repentance in this way – as a way of conversion – of turning away from ourselves and turning our hearts to God in love – we can perhaps understand why we cannot do it by ourselves, why we cannot "pull ourselves up by our own bootstraps." True repentance is always a sign of the presence of the Holy Spirit in us, and it is his work. The Gospel tells us that Christ's call to repentance – and that of John the Baptist before him – was made in the power of the Spirit (Luke 4: 14). We can only enter the way of repentance or persevere on it if we are summoned and sustained by the Holy Spirit. Repentance is the life of the Spirit within us, a life of truth and of love.

The Spirit of Truth makes it possible for us to face the truth of ourselves and of the world in which we live. As Jesus said, the Holy Spirit "convicts the world of sin" (John 16:8). Nonetheless, because he is also the Spirit of Love – our Advocate and Consoler – this "conviction" is not a sentence of death, but a call to conversion. We can return to God, be reconciled to him and receive his mercy and healing.

Repentance – conversion of the heart – does not mean being filled and tormented by guilt. Instead, it means being ready to admit our responsibility for our actions and our need for forgiveness, and having a firm desire to change our life: to turn away from ourselves in prayer and in love. Repentance means, above all, a constant, patient, growing in love. It means our willingness to open ourselves to the work of the Spirit in us and to embrace fully the gift of our salvation.

SALVATION

For many Christians, salvation seems to signify some future state of being "happy," of being in heaven, of being in no pain. It is largely a negative notion – of what it is not, rather than of what it is. Going to heaven is desirable, mainly because it saves us from going to hell. An old wise priest used to say that most Christians "back themselves into heaven." They are so preoccupied with trying to back away from hell, that they eventually "stumble backwards" into heaven!

In other words, salvation is often understood as a means to an end, a way of escaping hell, a "ticket" to heaven. To assure ourselves that we will acquire it, we think it is necessary to believe in a few required definitions, behave in a certain required way and follow the rules laid down for us. We are inclined to understand sin essentially as disobedience – breaking a commandment: we might be punished for it, so we should avoid it and regret it. It does not fill us with true sorrow and longing for "conversion" – our own change of heart. The very notion of repentance as a way of life – ceaseless repentance, as it was understood by the early Church – seems completely incomprehensible to us.

Yet the salvation which the Gospel proclaims, for which the martyrs died, and which the Church has taught from the beginning, is not a means to an end – a way of avoiding pain – but the end itself. It is the truth of who we really are and of what we can come to be. Salvation is a treasure beyond price, a pearl for which we are ready to give up all things. It is a gift of life – eternal, glorious, overflowing with love, radiant with joy, open to us now, this very moment, to embrace and to live. It alone fulfils all our desires, answers all our needs.

Salvation restores to us – today – the vision of God, the gift of his presence, which we were meant to enjoy every moment of our existence, and which, through the mystery of free will – of sin – humanity has lost or obscured. It opens to us, again, the gates of Paradise. Salvation – heaven – is simply, miraculously, participation in the life of God.

Breaking of the Heart

Seen from this perspective, the sin of which the Spirit "convicts the world" is much more than any specific wrong we may have committed or may commit, or even the sum total of them all. Sin, as the Tradition of the Church understands it, is the fundamental cause of all our individual sins, the source from which they all spring. Sin is the human condition, the state of separation from God.

It is from this sense of separation – alienation – that our repentance flows. We repent because, when we catch even the tiniest glimpse of God, of his perfection and beauty, we are filled with longing and love. At the same time, our hearts break with sadness, because we realize how far we are from this perfection and beauty, how far our world is from it, how separated from God, how bound by chains of blindness, imperfection and sin. And, above all, our hearts break because we realize that the source of this separation does not lie somewhere outside ourselves, but in our

11

hearts themselves: the chains that bind us are the chains of our own self-centredness – our preoccupation with self. Without this realization, without this breaking of the heart, there can be no true repentance.

It is not an easy way. The saints who have practised it have called it "white martyrdom" – the way of dying to sin. It is never easy to face our own inner confusion, our loneliness, our sense of alienation and guilt, our inability to love. It may be, at times, excruciatingly difficult to resist the temptation to protect ourselves from such self-knowledge, to justify ourselves and blame others. We become despondent and are tempted to despair. But we resist the temptation; we accept the call to conversion. As we enter the way of repentance, we face the truth of ourselves and surrender ourselves completely, weak sinners that we are, to the merciful love of God.

This is why repentance can also be called a way of "making friends" with ourselves, learning to accept ourselves as we are, without fear or guilt, without too much self-analysis or any self-pity. It is a way in which we can come to terms with our own inner darkness and realize that we do not need to hide from our weakness and sins. We know how to face and bear them and how to be freed from them. We can bring them all simply and openly to God, not so that he would "punish"

12

us, but that he may forgive and heal us. Repentance is the way of forgiveness and love.

ASKING FORGIVENESS

We have become so used to thinking of guilt as a negative and harmful emotion that we are prone to ignoring, even suppressing, every manifestation of it in ourselves. We cannot easily distinguish between "true" guilt – compunction – and the neurotic one. So, when we become aware of the wrongs we have done, we find it difficult to accept responsibility for them. We tend to justify our sinful actions as results of sins committed against us and, thus, strictly speaking, not our fault. We tend to believe that if we hate, it is because we have been hurt; if we cannot love, it is because we have not been loved; we resent, because we have never had our needs fulfilled. We prefer to think of ourselves as "wounded" – as victims of sin – rather than as sinners, and thus we do not often ask or want to be forgiven.

To ask for forgiveness implies an admission that, in fact, we have done something wrong, that we are in the wrong, and that, in some essential way, we are answerable for it. To admit the need for forgiveness requires that we no longer think of ourselves as victims of what has been done to us, of our past, but that we claim responsibility for what we do and who we are. This is surprisingly difficult for us. Our every instinct, every habit of thought fights against it. Still, it is the first essential step on the path of conversion, the beginning of our healing from guilt.

But how and of whom should we ask forgiveness? First of all, of course, we must ask forgiveness directly and personally of all those, alive or dead, against whom we have sinned, as Christ told us to do. We cannot go any further on the way of repentance unless we at least try to do that. If, for whatever reason, this is impossible for us, we must pray for those we have harmed, ask God to heal them, and thus turn the evil we have done to their good. If they are unable or unwilling to forgive us, we must ceaselessly pray that this grace may be given to them – not for the relief of our conscience, primarily, but above all for the sake of their own healing and peace.

The need for forgiveness, however, is not limited to forgiveness from those we have harmed. We must also ask to be forgiven by God. In the most fundamental sense, only God can forgive sins (cf. Mark 2:7). When we offend our neighbour, we offend God, and when we offend God, we always affect others. This is why true forgiveness is impossible outside a relationship with God. It is always a gift of his mercy. It is not as if there were two kinds for forgiveness: one from God, one from those we have harmed. Forgiveness is one big movement of grace, one big outpouring of the healing mercy of God. Human forgiveness is, perhaps one can say, a "sacramental" sign of the forgiveness of God, and in some mysterious way its necessary condition. Or, at least, our willingness to ask for the forgiveness of those against whom we have sinned seems to be a necessary condition of being able to receive the forgiveness of God.

FORGIVING OURSELVES

We hear a lot nowadays about the need to "forgive ourselves." We are told that such forgiveness is an essential step to our emotional and spiritual healing. Unless we forgive ourselves for our weaknesses and imperfections and stop accusing ourselves, we cannot let go of our fear and guilt and reach self-acceptance and inner peace.

It is no doubt true that, unless we accept ourselves and learn to love ourselves, we cannot ever be at peace. But how is it to be done? How do we forgive ourselves? Can we do it on our own? Should we turn to psychotherapy or other forms of counselling for help? Should we analyse ourselves, find out where our feelings of fear and guilt come from, and decide that from now on we shall be free of them? Will our negative emotions disappear if we find out what caused them, if we discover that we cannot be blamed for them?

Perhaps we have already tried that way of self-forgiveness. We may have gone to a therapist, joined a self-help group, or studied various methods of self-improvement on our own. We may have found some of these methods very helpful to us. We were able, perhaps, to shed the crushing burden of guilt we had carried since childhood, and to understand its causes. We may have discovered how to deal better with our painful negative emotions, and to be less compulsive in our behaviour. We may have learned to accept ourselves better. These are essential steps on our way to inner freedom and we should be grateful for them. Nevertheless, they cannot by themselves bring us to the final goal of our inner journey, which is much bigger than self-understanding and self-acceptance. It is bigger than self. It is a gift of God and we cannot reach it by ourselves, or with the help of any human therapy.

Our final goal is not self-improvement but self-surrender. Fullness of life – salvation – is our participation in the life of God and can only be found in a relationship with God. If it is true that only God can forgive sins, it must also be true that we cannot forgive ourselves. We can only ask for and receive forgiveness from God. It is only through repentance – through our willingness to open ourselves to God and trust in his mercy – that we can really know ourselves, accept ourselves and truly "forgive ourselves."

Forgiving Others

As we are forgiven, so must we forgive others. If we harbour our feelings of anger, resentment or hate, if we are unable or unwilling to forgive, it means that we are still only reacting to what others may have done to us. It means that we still think of ourselves as victims, we are not taking responsibility for ourselves and we are not free.

It is a fundamental principle of all spiritual life, I think, that our negative emotions – anger, hatred, envy or fear – are not simply imposed on us from outside, but find their source in our own hearts – that they express how we feel about ourselves and the world. We cannot hope to be freed from them, unless we "claim" them and assume responsibility for them. This does not mean that we should feel guilty for having these emotions or, God forbid, blame ourselves for the evil committed against us by others, as victims of abuse sometimes do. It only means that we realize that our negative and painful emotions are *our* emotions, and thus that we have a choice to allow them to take control over us or to refuse to act on them.

This is not always easy for us to see. When we are hurt by others, when some evil is done to us, it seems only natural to feel victimized, to hate, to blame. When we are pushed, it seems natural to want to push back in return. To choose not to do so, but to forgive and "turn the other cheek" may appear to be an invitation to more evil and a sign of weakness and cowardice. We tend to cherish our "righteous" anger and hate. We sometimes believe that to let go of them is not only unnatural, but may even be wrong. For much of its existence, including the present, most of humankind has considered anger and retribution not only normal, but a social and even a religious duty. Not to resist the aggressor, not to seek vengance for a wrong done against oneself, one's family, country or friends, is still often viewed as a failure of nerve and an offence against loyalty and honour.

And yet, it is this "failure" to which the Gospel calls us. The Gospel tells us that we cannot deal with evil by more evil, but only by forgiveness and love.That is the path that Christ walked and we must try to follow him on it, however difficult it seems to us, however often we stumble and fall. For only if we try to forgive our enemies, if we do not justify our negative feelings towards anybody but repent of them, can we be healed of our own darkness and pain.

REPENTING FOR OTHERS

Yet sometimes we may be asked to go even further than this on our way of repentance. Sometimes we may hear of some unspeakable evil committed by others – a murder, an abuse, a devastating war, or a genocide. It may happen close to us or in another part of the world. How can we come to terms with the knowledge that such things happen at all? Can we simply ignore them? Can we ever convince ourselves that they are "not our problem," not our fault and, therefore, not our concern? As Christians, can we ever find true peace unless we bring before God all the evils ever committed, surrender them to his mercy, and ask his forgiveness? Unless we repent for them?

At first, repenting for evil committed by others may make little sense to us. Our fundamental sense of justice seems to rebel against such a possibility. But we must remind ourselves that repentance is not bearing guilt, but calling for mercy and healing. In that light, repenting for the sins of others – atoning for them – asking God to change their hearts and heal them, is simply another way, perhaps the only way, of loving them. It may also be the way of helping, in a small measure, to heal the evil they have brought upon the world. We do not need to *feel* kind and loving towards them, we do not need to *feel* sorry for them. All we must do is to pray for them. If we find even that unbearably difficult, we might find it helpful to remember that every day we too add, however little, to the sum of the world's sin. Only God can ever know what great evil might yet result from all the "little" evils we have done, what will be the final outcome of our lack of love, our resentments or our fears.

Yet we must also remember that, when we repent for the sins of others, that is, those not committed against ourselves, we are not "absolving" their sin; we are not forgiving them. We have no right to forgive what we have not suffered, horrors we have not gone through and which, perhaps, we could not forgive if we had. Nonetheless, we can pray to God to give the evildoers the grace to repent so that he can forgive them. We must pray for their victims, too – the living and the dead – that the grace of forgiveness may be given to them, that they may be healed of their pain, their anger and their hate, and that they may be at peace. Thus the evil done to them may also be turned into good and be deprived of its victory.

Victory over Evil

There is no greater victory of evil than the reaction of guilt and despair which it arouses in those who have committed a sin, or of fear, anger and hate in those who have been wronged. Conversely, there is no greater victory over evil than to refuse to give in to these feelings, to refuse to act on them, to harbour them or justify them. We defeat evil – in ourselves, in others or in the world – when we refuse to react to it with more evil, but respond to it with repentance, forgiveness and love.

We often think that Christ conquered evil by his physical suffering on the cross, by his agony and pain. This is not true, strictly speaking. Christ conquered evil when he refused to resist or hate his tormentors, but forgave them and prayed for them. Christ won his victory by love and we must try to do the same. Mother Maria Gysi, an Orthodox nun who died in England in 1977, used to say that when we refuse to give in to guilt and despair, but throw ourselves on the mercy of God, or when we refuse to resist and hate our enemies, but forgive and pray for them, we "dis-evil" the evil which we have done or which has been done to us. We remove its "sting," and we vanquish it by turning it into good.[1] This is the only "war" with evil to which the Gospel calls us, this is our true work in the world, our participation in the work of the world's salvation.

But how can this work be accomplished? How can we obey this call, or win this victory in a "real" world in which there are people, including most often ourselves, who do fail in love, who do hurt others, who hate, rob and kill? In a world in which there are wars, wicked governments and awful weapons, how can we refuse to protect the innocent and the weak? Can we "forgive" the murderers and let them go free? Can we refuse to resist an aggressor? Is the use of force never justified? Is war always wrong?

These are real, terrible questions and no Christian can avoid facing them, but each has to face them alone. We cannot solve the problem of evil for anybody else, or have the right to impose our own solution on anybody else. We cannot demand non-resistance of others, however clear it may seem to us that the Gospel calls us to it. We cannot demand it of our governments, we cannot demand it even of the Church. We cannot demand it of ourselves, unless we can embrace it out of love. Always, the weak – and this means most of us – must be protected, or the fruit of evil will be even more evil: more human suffering, more fear and despair. It may seem clear to us at times that resistance is the lesser of two evils, that "turning the other cheek" may be an act of cowardice, a refusal to help a neighbour and a failure of love.

In such situations there can be no clear solution. We can never be sure if the course we choose is right. We can never foresee the consequences which our actions may bring upon ourselves and the world. Yet, one thing, I think, is clear: each violent act, each movement of anger or hate, however good the reason for it may appear to be, brings with it much evil and pain and adds to the ocean of suffering present in the world. There are no holy wars. This is why early Christians considered it necessary to repent for any act of violence they had committed, however justified or "legal" it seemed. Perhaps they understood better than we can, that no act of violence was ever free from sin, and should always evoke in us a deep sorrow and heart-felt repentance.

Victory over evil has already been won on the cross. Yet our own participation in that victory – responding to evil with love – is a hard task and does not happen overnight. For a long time, maybe all our lives, we must struggle with our fears and resentments, our inability to forgive, our compulsion to blame and hate. We may be driven by our emotions and feel unworthy of love, feel we are no good. Nevertheless, on a deeper level, we are already at peace, because we have begun to believe in God's mercy and to open ourselves to it in repentance. We have begun to believe in the final victory of love in ourselves, as well as in the world. This is the essence of faith – of trust – and we must hold on to it, whatever our emotions, fears or doubts.

TRUST

St. Paul tells us that God loves us even before we repent, "while we are still in our sins" (Romans 5:8). This is another way of saying that God never ceases to love us. God's loving mercy is infinite, it knows no limits, it lays down no conditions. The only thing that can prevent it from flowing over us, from healing us, is our failure to trust it. It is we who put limitations upon the mercy of God, we who cannot believe that there is nothing we can or must do to "deserve" it, that it is given to us unconditionally and is totally free. In other words, we are afraid that God's mercy, like ours, is finite and can fail. As we shall see, it is this fear, our failure to trust, which is the "root" of all our sin.

Sometimes when we say that we trust God, we mean that we believe he will help us in our troubles, answer all our prayers and look after all our needs. In other words, we mean that he will save us from suffering and death. Our trust, however, must be bigger than that. We must also trust God

29

when suffering overwhelms us, when our prayers seem unanswered and our needs unfulfilled. Can we do that? Can we trust God when he seems forever absent from our lives, when he seems to have abandoned his world? Can we trust him when we hear of some dreadful evil, a natural disaster, an epidemic, a tragic death, for which there is nobody on this earth to blame? Can we still believe in his love? Can we trust God blindly, "madly," as St. Therese of Lisieux liked to say?

To trust God unconditionally means to believe that no evil in the world, no evil in us or in any other human being, no disaster or tragedy, can ever prevent his mercy from being poured out on us. Above all, it means to stand before him in all our weakness and sin and to trust that he will never reject us, however greatly and often we may have sinned; that "neither death, nor life, nor angels, nor principalities, nor present things, nor future things nor height, nor depth, nor any other creature will be able to separate us from the love of God in Christ Jesus our Lord" (Romans 8:38-39).

Yet, how can we believe it? We have nothing in our human experience to compare to such love, to tell us what it is like. In our heart of hearts we know that nobody in this world, not even the most loving of parents or the best of friends, could love us like that. We know that we could not love like that. We know that all human love has a limit and can end. Death, separation, our own sin – the core of selfishness present in the heart of every person in this life – can weaken or destroy it. Therefore we cannot even imagine with our finite minds what God's infinite love for us means. We cannot make ourselves believe in it; we cannot trust it totally, unconditionally – in the face of all the evil and suffering we see in the world or find lurking in our own hearts. Such faith and trust are given only to the saints.

Blessed Elizabeth of the Trinity (a Carmelite nun who lived in France at the turn of the century) once wrote in *Praise of Glory* that God loved everybody, but only saints really believed it. Saints are not those who are always "good," who are "sinless," but those who, certain of God's love, can be totally open to the truth of their being; totally real, they do not need to justify themselves in any way, to hide or to pretend. Saints are unafraid and free.

Saints have the grace to hold onto their trust in God whatever evil they may encounter, and whatever suffering they must undergo, because they know that God's love is infinite. They know, therefore, that the ultimate answer to the mystery of suffering must also be love. Such trust may not be given to us: we may never be able to experience it in this life. Still, we can always pray for it and in love and repentance surrender our weakness to God.

LOST PARADISE

The weakness of our trust in God and our tendency to doubt his love for us spring from the underlying ground of all sin: the state of separation from God in which humanity has been since the Fall. According to the biblical account (Genesis 2), when Adam and Eve sinned, they lost their vision of God, his beauty, his perfection and his merciful love. Whether we take this account literally or in its symbolic sense, the truth expressed in it is central to understanding the nature of human sin and of the Christian need of repentance. The essence of our parents' "fall" was not that they broke a specific commandment, but that they failed to trust God. Having experienced God's friendship and love, surrounded as they were by the beauty and goodness of his creation, they listened to the voice of the Adversary, who accused God of jealousy and deception: of forbidding them to reach for the fruit of the knowledge of good and evil in order to protect his own power!

It is hard for us to understand how Adam and Eve could have done that, how they could have chosen to believe the devil rather than God. But they did, and in this lies the mystery of human freedom. Because of that choice, sin entered the world and the unity of all things was broken. Our first parents became estranged from God, from each other and from the rest of creation; they became fragmented in themselves and afraid. Because they had lost trust in God's love, they did not ask for his forgiveness, but hid from him, blamed each other for their sin and were banished from Paradise.

> When God calls Adam, far from crying out with horror and throwing himself before his creator, he accuses the woman. . . . Man, therefore, refuses his responsibility, throws it onto the woman and finally on God Himself. . . . Man is not free, [Man himself] lets it be understood; creation, therefore God, has led him to evil. [2]

This is the true meaning of the Fall and the source of our sense of separation from God. The Fall is ours, too, because all of us inherit the consequences of our first parents' sin – not necessarily their sin, but its consequences. Sometimes we find this difficult to accept, we rebel against it, we think that it is not fair. Nevertheless it is surely so. We see the truth of it in our everyday world, in which we all carry the burden of our parents' sins and our children so often must suffer for ours. This is another painful way in which we experience the mystery of evil in our own lives and are challenged to repentance and trust.

THE ROOT OF SIN

If we think again of this fundamental nature of the Fall – our first parents' failure to trust God – we see at once the most important result of the Fall for them, and, consequently, for us, too. As soon as Adam and Eve failed in their trust in God and were unable to admit responsibility for their sin and ask forgiveness for it, they became "afflicted," weighed down with guilt. They turned away from God and became centred on themselves. We too must carry the same burden. All our lives, we must struggle not only with fear and guilt, but also with a compulsion to justify ourselves, to hide from the world and even from God.

It is our failure of trust, our turning away from God and focusing on ourselves – our self-centredness – our need to protect ourselves at all cost, which the Fathers considered the root of all our sin. Because we are unable to trust anybody, or anything, and, above all else, because we are not able to trust God, we are compelled to rely on our own resources, to attempt to find our own happiness, and to fulfil our own desires and needs. We are imprisoned, stranded on the island of our self. We are all exiles from Paradise.

It is from the sin of self-centredness that Christ came to deliver us. This is why he insisted so emphatically on the primacy of the commandment of love. Love is our only door to heaven, because only love can break the chains of self-centredness and separation from God, which define hell. When we love God above all else and our neighbour as ourselves, we forget ourselves, we die to self and we are made free. By loving, we grow into Christ – the God-Man – who has in himself rejoined heaven and earth and put an end to our separation from God. But we must grow into him – we must learn to love: this is the task to which we have all been called, but at which we most often fail. Therefore, we must ceaselessly repent.

CEASELESS REPENTANCE

Ceaseless repentance flows from our realization that we belong to God: his beauty and glory are our home (though we are exiled from it), and between us and God there is an abyss, which of ourselves we cannot cross. God is infinite, we are finite; he is perfect, we are sinners; he is eternal, we are under a sentence of death. A life of repentance means a constant awareness of the reality of our condition, a willingness to face ourselves as we really are. At the same time, it means a total openness to the reality of God's presence and of his tender, forgiving love.

In the words of Fr. Alexander Schmemann, ceaseless repentance is "a mysterious mixture of despair and hope, of darkness and light."[3] The essence of this hope lies in our faith that this infinite, unreachable God has made himself "reachable," that he has come to us, and in Christ has made himself available to us. He has crossed the abyss and stands waiting to take us to the other side. We do not need to do anything but call to him for mercy and love. Ceaseless repentance is the way in which all of us, however sinful or "holy," can experience, moment by moment, his mercy and love.

We tend to say "mercy and love" as if they were two separate things, yet they are not two, but one. God's mercy is his love for us: this is the way in which God loves us and the only way in which we can receive his love. Mother Maria used to say that if God had not "dimmed" the burning glory of his love, if he had not "contained" it, we could not have borne it. If he revealed himself to us in all his beauty and glory, if he poured his divine love on us in all its infinite power, it would have crushed us; we would have "dissolved" completely into him and ceased to exist. So, "it pleased God to love us carefully," in a "beggar's cloak" of human flesh, so that we could receive it and open ourselves to it without fear.[4] It is this "careful love" which we mean by mercy. When we repent, when we ask for mercy, we are asking only for love.

Even when we love another human being and know we are loved, we so often feel "unworthy," amazed at the gift which has been bestowed on us, and which, we realize, we can never "deserve." How much more so in our relationship with God! The more we love him and long for him, the more we grieve over our "unworthiness" and our separation from him. This is why it has always been true that it is the saints, the purest of heart, the ones least burdened with sin, who always repent the most. It is not because they think or imagine that they have outdone us all in sinning, but because they have eyes to see what it is they long for and what they cannot, in this life, ever fully possess.

MIRROR OF PERFECTION

If it is difficult for most of us to understand the acuteness of the saints' longing and pain, perhaps it is because we only rarely glimpse what they clearly saw – their own inadequacy before the glorious beauty of the face of Christ. As Christians, we believe that the perfection of God is fully mirrored in the person of Christ, that Christ is the perfect reflection of the beauty and glory of God. We do not often realize, however, that in the person of Christ we also have the perfect mirror of our own nature as God intended it to be, and the perfect measure of the holiness to which he has called us.

When Christ commanded us to be like God, as perfect as God, he gave us the Gospel as the measure of this perfection. If we could live the Gospel perfectly, we would indeed be "perfect as our Heavenly Father is perfect." We would love as Christ did; we would be holy like him. Yet we cannot live it, however much we may desire it, and however hard we try. Each day, each moment, each attempt to live like Christ did brings to mind this truth. Evil which we encounter at each step, our own need to protect ourselves, our fear, force us to a daily compromise. The Gospel is a mirror in which we see God, but also ourselves as we truly are. We cannot live by divine measures: we are too small, too weak. We fail again and again, and thus we must repent. The Gospel is a measure of our failure and a call to repentance.

For many of us this seems an impossible, even absurd, demand. It appears to ask us to repent for the mere fact of being human – for not being angels – for being as God made us to be. It suggests that God has called us to a way of life, a "state of perfection," which he knew we could never attain. For some of us, this recalls the terrible burden of guilt imposed on us in our early years, when we were blamed for things we could not help, things often done to us. It may bring back a childhood sense of inadequacy, when we were expected to do things we were just not capable of, or things we were too frightened to achieve. Of course, this may sometimes be so: we may be expecting too much of ourselves, despising ourselves for not being perfect, for not being "saints." This would be pride – the greatest of sins – and we must always be on guard against it.

When we say, however, that the Gospel is "a measure of our failure and a call to repentance," we do not mean that we should blame ourselves for being human and hate ourselves for not being "perfect," as we think we should be. We only mean that we should realize ever more fully that we are imperfect and far from being saints, that we have not yet "arrived," but are still on the way. Trying to live the Gospel is a very humble path, a path on which we can never fully "succeed," from which we constantly turn away, and to which, therefore, we must constantly return. It is the negative path of daily conversion.

THE NEGATIVE WAY

We can never "achieve" perfection. We cannot achieve perfect prayer, perfect trust, perfect forgiveness or perfect love. We cannot have one totally unselfish thought, emotion or act. We cannot really be "good," for only God is good (Mark 10:19). The key to holiness lies in our realizing this fact and accepting it gladly, without fear. This is the true grace of repentance. Mother Maria often pointed out this truth and referred to it as a "negative way" of perfection. When we learn to accept and to face our weakness, our imperfection, we witness to the fact that perfection does exist. Otherwise, we could not repent for failing to reach it. Yet we also witness to the fact that it exists only and fully in God. And we realize that when we repent of our lack of it, suddenly perfection is within our grasp.

We reach perfection, perhaps only for a moment, "in one swoop," negatively, by repenting of our inability to reach it.[5] As soon as we acknowledge our sin, as soon as we re-turn to God and beg his forgiveness for it, we are immediately healed of it, we are made "perfect," whole, as we are meant to be. Our inability to stay healed does not change this fact, but only means that we must never cease to repent. Repentance is, as it were, our "shortcut to perfection."

This may seem to many people a strange and distorted way of looking for holiness. By constantly dwelling on the negative, dark side of our nature, how can we ever get past it and learn that at the centre of our being there are also goodness and love? Would it not be better to concentrate on the positive?

It is true, of course, that we need to be aware of our positive side, of our inherent goodness and beauty as God intended us to be. We need to recall that, in a fundamental, essential way, we are "OK." On the other hand, it is not our goodness which prevents us from being truly ourselves, and cuts us off from each other and from God! It is our sense of guilt, our awareness of evil and suffering which exist in ourselves and in the world. It is the difficulty we have believing in God's love for us as we are. It is our preoccupation with self and our inability to love. It is only when we face these feelings, whenever they arise, when we weed them from our hearts and allow God's mercy to take root in us, that we find the door to holiness – fullness of being.

I heard somebody say once that it did not really matter how often and how miserably we failed in our search for perfection; what mattered was how quickly we realized that we had failed and how quickly we were willing to try again. This, I think, is very true. When we become aware that, once again, we have failed to live out the call of the Gospel – failed to love, to forgive, to pray, to serve – we do not get angry at ourselves, blame ourselves for being weak, or try to justify ourselves by blaming others. We do not think of ourselves at all. We turn away from self, we die to self, we throw ourselves onto the mercy of God and we simply repent. The way of repentance is the way of love, and love always unites us with God. The perfection for which we long – our only perfection – does not lie in our being as perfect as God, but only in being one with God. There is nothing else we can desire or need, and nothing else that can give us greater joy.

THE GREATEST JOY

The joy of repentance cannot be "proven" by reason, experienced in our emotions or explained in
words. When we begin to walk the way of repentance, we must simply believe that this joy is real
and that it is a gift which God means us to have.
We believe it, because it is the message of the
Gospel and has been witnessed to and taught by
the saints. For the saints, however hard they
grieved over their human condition, however
hard they repented, also had the gift of joy. A joy-
less saint is an impossibility, a contradiction in
terms, perhaps even a fraud.

The saints' source of joy was not a conviction
of having reached perfection, and, therefore, of
having nothing of which to repent – how absurd it
would be to assume that. Rather, it was their as-
surance that their weakness or the most grievous
of sins could not separate them from the love of
God. The saints, perhaps, really understood what
St. Paul meant when he said that "strength was

made perfect in weakness" (2 Corinthians 12:9), and believed that the humble carrying of their sins and imperfections in repentance brought them most closely to the perfection and holiness of God. Repentance was the saints' meeting with God. There can be no greater joy.

Through repentance, we too can receive again and again the mercy of God and experience the reality of his presence. We too are able to break the chains of self-protection and learn that, before the face of God, not even the darkest corner of our being need be hidden or denied. Perhaps we cannot imitate the saints' greatness or their works, practise the same discipline or reach the same spiritual heights. Nonetheless, each of us, in the measure given to us by God, can walk the same way of repentance and share in the same joy.

PRACTICE OF REPENTANCE

The way of repentance has been taught to us and lived by the saints. We know that we should repent for our sins. We know that it is not a way of guilt, but of love. Sometimes, however, we do not clearly understand how we can repent "ceaselessly" – how we can make repentance a part of our ordinary lives, how we can live it. As it needs to be said again and again, repentance is a grace from God, a gift of the Holy Spirit, and of ourselves we cannot "achieve" it. Yet this is not the whole answer. We too must do our part, we must work at it, however pitiful and unimportant our efforts may seem to us.

How, then, do we "work" at repentance? Is there a path we can walk, a discipline we should follow, prayers we must say? Is there anything at all that we must do to learn repentance? To this there is no one answer. There is no single way which everybody must follow. We must pray about it, seek spiritual guidance and learn from the experience of others. Again, because repentance is the work of the Spirit within us, in the end only he can show us which way is best for us.

For those of us who belong to the Catholic and Orthodox Traditions, the most obvious, direct way of repentance – of asking God's forgiveness – is to go to confession. Yet it is important to remember that sacramental confession, although it is and must always be an expression of our repentance and a sign of God's mercy, is not the only way we can ask and receive forgiveness from God.

The repentance of which the Fathers and Mothers of both Traditions spoke is not an individual spiritual act, however sacred and necessary, but a way of constant, humble awareness of our weakness and sin, of our separation from God. It is a ceaseless cry for forgiveness and love. We are not discouraged by any lack of feeling or absence of tears. We do not worry whether we are "successful" or not. Most likely we are not. It is this trying, these pitiful attempts at repenting that are, I think, our true practice of repentance.

The practice of repentance has been described as "weeding our patch" – the little piece of ground which God gave each one of us to cultivate. God has already sown on it the seeds of salvation, of goodness and of eternal life. We cannot prevent weeds of sin and self-centredness from growing up on it. We must not worry and despise ourselves too much if they do – this is the human condition, the law of life in this world. We should not pull them out too roughly, and we must always be watchful, lest we pull out the good with the bad (Matthew 13:29). We weed our patch peacefully, carefully, and we do not get discouraged because there is never an end to our task.

PENANCE

Sometimes, we need to express our repentance and our longing for conversion by undertaking some form of penance and self-denial. We may try to "mortify" ourselves a little: pray more, fast, give up a pleasure, share some of our resources or control our appetites. Penance strengthens our will and makes us more aware of our weakness and our total dependence on God. It is essential, however, never to impose any extraordinary penances on ourselves or attempt any heroic measures without the guidance of an experienced spiritual director. Such attempts may be an expression of true repentance, of love and longing for God, but they may also be a result of a disturbed mind or spiritual pride. We should not trust our own judgement in this.

We should also not confuse penance with repentance. Repentance is an attitude of mind and a way of life, a path of conversion, while penance is only one of the means we may use to follow it.

Penance without true repentance makes no sense at all, but there can be true repentance without any external acts of penance.

The same should be said of asceticism – a way of severe mortification and austerity often embraced by holy men and women, especially in the past. Some of us may find ourselves attracted to it; in others, perhaps in most, it evokes doubt and even fear. We should not let ourselves be troubled by this. Asceticism – the term originally referred to the training of athletes before a competition – was a way in which some men and women tried to train themselves for battle against their own weakness and the power of evil in the world. These were the great "athletes" of God. We should not try to imitate them; we should not try to imitate anybody, however revered and holy they were. What was asked of them may very well not be asked of us. We cannot "elect" ourselves for greatness.

In our own lives, any training we really need will most likely come our way without any special effort on our part to find it. The demands of everyday Christian life, the challenge of following Christ and living the life of the Gospel, our daily dying to self, will be penance enough for most of us. It will always be the means not of punishment, but of healing; it will always bring us back to the only thing that matters: a deeper realization of God's infinite mercy and of our great need of it. A sign of true conversion is not our "self-improvement," or the length of our prayers, or the severity of our penances, but our growth in love.

THE JESUS PRAYER

One of the best-known ways of prayer and repentance in the Orthodox Tradition, and one becoming familiar also to many Christians of the West, is the ancient practice of the Jesus Prayer. It consists of constant, patient, silent repetition of the words "Lord Jesus Christ, Son of God, have mercy on me, a sinner!" or "Lord Jesus Christ, have mercy on me!" or even "Lord, have mercy!" Sometimes only the name of Jesus is invoked, over and over again, not with our lips, but in our hearts.

We practise the Jesus Prayer simply by saying it every day, as often as we can, as often as we remember to say it. At first, this practice may seem to us too monotonous, too boring, too "dry," and we may not find much joy in it. If we persevere, however, and if it is the will of God for us and the work of the Holy Spirit, we shall find joy: the Prayer eventually will become part of our own being, our own cry of trust and love. We will find that it goes on within us wherever we are and whatever we do, whether we are fully aware of it or not. It will become the background to our whole life. It will become for us the way of ceaseless prayer about which St. Paul wrote (2 Thessalonians 5:17), and of ceaseless repentance.

The Jesus Prayer is always a prayer of love and repentance. It focuses our attention on the Person of Christ our Saviour: it is said to him and in his presence; it acknowledges his lordship and his power; it calls on his mercy; and it helps us to open our hearts to him. It is a perfect expression of our trust in his merciful love. This is why the Jesus Prayer has been called "a summary of the Gospel," a confession of faith in our salvation in Christ. Each time we call on his name we testify to our conviction that he will save and forgive us, that he will heal us and pour all his love, all his tender mercy upon us, however often we fail, however terrible our sins.

> Praying the Holy Name, we pray the whole Gospel, we place ourselves in it and live it more and more until it becomes our very own life, our hope and our true end wherein death turns into life.[6]

Praying the Jesus Prayer is not the only way to practise repentance. It may be the best way for us, but we should never try to impose it on others. The heart of all true repentance, the heart of all true prayer, is a longing and a search for the presence of God with us, before the eyes of our soul, at the very centre of our being. So we must not worry too much how we should repent but only ceaselessly seek God's presence in prayer. All true prayer will, sooner or later, lead us to repentance, for when we have glimpsed, even for a moment, the beauty and glory of God in the face of Christ, we shall know what true repentance is and why we can never stop practising it.

THE GIFT OF TEARS

Some people receive the grace to know God's mercy in their bodies, as well as in their hearts. This is the gift of tears. In the tradition of the Orthodox Church, this gift, although not given to many, holds a very important place. It appears at the very birth of Christianity in the tears of the woman who wept at the feet of Christ out of sorrow for her sinful past, but also out of her great love and joy for being forgiven. They are the tears of the Apostle Peter, after he had denied Christ, when the Lord turned and looked at him. Many stories of the great saints of the desert attest to the reality of this gift and its significance.

The gift of tears is always understood as an expression of deep sorrow for sin and of great longing for God. Tears of repentance are often referred to as a "second baptism": some believe that they wash away our sins, re-unite us with Christ, and restore us to the life of Paradise. Thus these tears of love and joy resemble the action of sacramental confession and are a source of grace.

The gift of tears was not only given in the past: some experience it today. We may have seen them ourselves on the faces of men and women attending a Liturgy, when kissing the holy icons or praying their "beads." Some have tried to describe their experience, because they realized that, although we cannot "acquire" or imitate this gift, we can still learn some important truths from those who have received it. As Catherine Doherty wrote:

> I weep and the tears wash away my sins and the sins of others. My mind is serene and unaffected, because I know that the grace of tears is not from my mind, but proceeds from the heart of God. It comes to my heart, and I weep. . . . You must never forget that when I weep, Christ weeps, because Christ is in me. When my tears mingle with those of Christ, then his holiness washes me, not mine. . . . The tears wash away my sins and the sins of the world. . . .[7]

The gift of tears, like any other exceptional spiritual gift, is a special grace, a gift of the Spirit, given to some for reasons known only to God. We cannot make ourselves cry like this. In fact, most spiritual fathers and mothers warn us not to try. If we do, the tears we might be able to produce would hardly be a sign of grace, but of self-centred emotionalism and a danger to our souls. For most of us, repentance will never be experienced in such an extraordinary way, but will always remain a path of discipline and constant effort: our work of love.

MEETING WITH DEATH

When repentance becomes for us a ceaseless attitude of spirit, a way of our life with God, it will also become our way of preparing for death, our "practice" for death. There is really no better way. At that unknown, mysterious moment when we are summoned to cross the boundary between time and eternity, between heaven and earth, and to meet Christ our God and our Judge at last, what else can we do but repent?

We shall be judged according to "heavenly measures," which we cannot begin to understand in this world, and by God, whose perfection we cannot begin to imagine, before whose face we have nothing to offer but our weakness and our prayer for mercy. Nonetheless, though our human nature may quake with fear, our hearts will be at peace. Our patient, daily practice of repentance will have taught us already that, in the presence of the infinite love of God, we do not need to do anything but trust in his mercy. We will have learned already that all of us, saints and sinners, can enter Paradise only like the Good Thief, through the mercy of Christ.

This is true not only of the moment of our physical death, but also of each moment of our existence. Each time we call "Lord have mercy on me a sinner!" we place ourselves in a position in which his mercy can reach us. We adopt the attitude of the Good Thief, who recognized the Lord in the man on the cross, and who therefore entered that very day with him into Paradise (Luke 23:43).

The death we must undergo, and which we must "practise," is our "daily death," the death of self to which every Christian is called. We must die to self in order that we may rise with Christ to new life. It is a daily death: we cannot do it all at once, but die and rise every moment of our lives. Through repentance we meet this death moment by moment and "turn it into life." We follow Christ, we surrender our self to him, we let it die so that

> it might rise again as unceasing repentance and compassion. It is here that we probably come nearest to understanding the continual call to repentance in the Orthodox Church. It is, on the one hand, like an alarm signal to be on our guard against our lower faculties, and on the other, a trumpet call for their resurrection.[8]

DEATH OF SIN

Repentance is a sure way in which we can share, in this life, in Christ's death and resurrection. As the Church has taught from the beginning, when we were baptised we were "buried with Christ" so that we could rise with him and live with him his risen life. As long as we are on earth, we carry the consequences of our first parents' sin, we are still exiles. Awareness of this truth makes us sad, but we do not despair, because we have also learned that repentance is the means by which the grace of baptism is restored to us. In this way, we "bury" our sins, not in the sense of denying them, but in the sense of surrendering them all to Christ. When we repent, we place our sins in his tomb, we die to them, and thus we rise from them. We rise again with Christ to new life, we are transformed into him – divinized, in the language of the Orthodox Church – and we return with him to Paradise.

Thus, our failures, our weaknesses, even our sins, through ceaseless repentance may become for us moments of grace and conversion of heart. They may become not obstacles but stepping stones to perfection, our discipline of love. We have nothing to fear. We look at the face of Christ; in the light of his mercy, our sins disappear like mist. They do not matter. Repentance is the death of sin, the death of the old, and the birth of the new. It is the one sure way in which we can live the life of Paradise already in this world, experiencing the fruits of our salvation. For when we repent, we place all our trust not in any "goodness" of our own, but in the mercy of God which can never fail us.

LIBERATION FROM SELF

Now we begin to see why repentance is a uniquely Christian path of liberation from self. All great religious traditions recognize that the deepest desire of the human heart is for freedom from inner oppression. We feel "conditioned": bound by the chains of our habits and compulsions, our likes and dislikes, our fears and guilt, our inability to love. Our great tragedy is that we so often mistake these habits and compulsions for our true self. Perhaps most of us operate on the assumption that this conditioned, unfree self is all there is, all we can ever be, and we fear that without it we could not exist at all. We are unable, therefore, to stop protecting ourselves at all cost. This fear, however, is an illusion and we need to be freed from it. Our false self must die, so that we can find our true self, the self which God meant us to be and which he created in his image and likeness.

Yet even when we begin to understand this, we tend to think that we must first of all know what our true self is; that we must understand it and have the way to it clearly marked for us. We search for this knowledge everywhere, we read books, we run after "gurus" who might be able to enlighten us. This is not the way, however. We cannot ever fully know, and nobody in this world can tell us, what our true self is. Like the "pearl of great price," it is buried in the depths of our heart and remains always beyond the grasp of our mind. We cannot fathom it ourselves or explain it to another. Yet we can live it, moment by moment, by repentance.

Our true self exists, but we cannot see it: it is too big for us and obscured by our sins and illusions. We can only uncover it by pulling out the weeds of untruth in us. This, again, is the "negative way" of repentance. When we repent, we surrender our false self into the hands of God, we die to it daily. We give up our illusions, our compulsions, our self-centredness as soon as we notice them; we cry for mercy and we always go on. We don't expect any quick answers or ask for any revelations. We look only to Christ our Lord and follow him step by step, and then, perhaps, in a few years, or in many – in God's own good time – we look around us and see that we have arrived; we are at the centre of things, we are true, simple and free. We have found our true self.

In the Christian Tradition, this true self is called the heart, and is understood as the very centre of our being – the "wide and open land" as

Mother Maria used to call it – where we are truly ourselves and where we meet God. This land and this meeting are, I think, what Jesus pointed to, when he blessed the "pure of heart." The pure of heart are those who, having turned away from themselves, are able to see God in themselves, in others, in the whole of creation and, therefore, are able to love themselves and their neighbour "even in their sins." The pure of heart are merciful and compassionate: they do not judge themselves or others; they have learned the meaning of love.

TRUE REPENTANCE

True repentance, then, is not an expression of fear, self-hate or of a neurotic sense of guilt, but an ordinary, simple, natural way of loving God. It is a meeting with God, who has loved us infinitely, whom we love and whose beauty and perfection we long to see, from whom we are separated by sin.

True repentance, holy repentance, is the way of love. It is only possible when we stand before the face of God and are moved "out of our minds," beyond the confines of our little narrow selves, by our longing for him. We long for him and search for his presence not because he can give us this or that, nor because he can save us from disaster and death, nor even because he can save us from hell. We long for him because he is so incomparably good and beautiful that, sinners as we are, we must long for him.

The secret of true repentance is humility, a spontaneous response of the human heart in the presence of God. Before him we are as small as a grain of dust; we have offended him again and again; nonetheless, he has come to us and loved us unto death.

Each time we call on the Lord to have mercy on us, we surrender ourselves to him, we accept his judgement and meet him already, as it were, at our end, at the moment of death. We face our fear of death, but also begin to experience the "indescribable and glorious joy" of our resurrection (1 Peter 1:3-9). While still on earth, we have already begun our life in heaven where, fully transformed into Christ and glorified with him, fully free, we know, at last, how infinitely we have been loved, how safe we have always been, how sure is our hope of reaching our true home. This is the true way of repentance and source of all our joy.

NOTES

1 Mother Maria, *The Hidden Treasure* (Toronto: Peregrina Publishing Co., 1991), p. 33.

2 Vladimir Lossky, *Orthodox Theology* (Crestwood, New York: St. Vladimir's Seminary Press, 1989), p. 82.

3 Fr. Alexander Schmemann, *Great Lent* (Crestwood, New York: St. Vladimir's Seminary Press, 1990), p. 28.

4 Mother Maria, *The Hidden Treasure*, p. 33.

5 Mother Maria, *Eastern Spirituality* (Toronto: Peregrina Publishing Co., 1992), p. 7.

6 Sister Theckla, ed., *Mother Maria, Her Life in Letters* (London: Darton, Longman and Todd, 1979), p. 47.

7 Catherine Doherty, *Poustinia ("The Desert")* (Notre Dame, Ind.: Ave Maria Press, 1975), p. 118.

8 Mother Maria, *The Jesus Prayer* (Toronto: Peregrina Publishing Co., 1991), p. 19.

Praise for Irma Zaleski's

Living the Jesus Prayer

(Novalis, Gracewing)

"With refreshing common sense, Zaleski describes the desire, the method, and the guidance that lead a person to the goal of all prayer."
Canadian Catholic Review

"The book serves three novel purposes. First, It allows Zaleski to tell the story of how she came to learn and recite the Jesus Prayer. Second, it gives her an opportunity to give a short history of the Jesus Prayer. Third, it lets her go through the technique of the prayer and show how it works."
BC Catholic

"Inspiring and encouraging . . ."
Fr. Thomas Hopko
Dean, St. Vladimir's
Orthodox Theological Seminary

"These words, clothed in the tenderness of Christ, will bring his merciful love to many . . ."
Fr. Robert Pelton
Madonna House

AGMV
MARQUIS
Québec, Canada
1999